50 Classic Dishes Reinvented

By: Kelly Johnson

Table of Contents

- Modern Meatloaf
- Fusion Mac and Cheese
- Global Chicken Pot Pie
- Spiced-Up Shepherd's Pie
- Deconstructed Lasagna
- Reimagined Caesar Salad
- Smoky Beef Stroganoff
- Korean-Inspired Sloppy Joes
- Vegan Bolognese
- Exotic Clam Chowder
- Bold Beef Wellington
- Mediterranean Ratatouille
- French Onion Tartlets
- Elevated Tuna Casserole
- Spicy Chili con Carne
- Global Pad Thai
- Garlic Butter Chicken Alfredo
- Japanese Curry Shepherd's Pie
- Creamy Mushroom Risotto
- Caribbean Jerk Roast Chicken
- Fresh Caprese Pizza
- Gourmet Grilled Cheese
- Thai Red Curry Meatballs
- Spinach and Feta Spanakopita
- Sweet Potato Gnocchi
- Roasted Eggplant Moussaka
- Tex-Mex Tacos al Pastor
- Peruvian-Inspired Ceviche
- Pineapple Fried Rice
- Coconut Chicken Korma
- Lemongrass Pho
- Cuban Sandwich Casserole
- Greek-Style Stuffed Peppers
- Sweet and Sour Pork Reimagined
- Butter Poached Lobster Rolls

- Moroccan-Spiced Tagine
- Middle Eastern Shakshuka
- Pesto Zucchini Noodles
- Tangy BBQ Pulled Jackfruit
- French-Inspired Quiche Lorraine
- Chorizo and Black Bean Stew
- Sweet Potato Shepherd's Pie
- Chili Lime Shrimp Tacos
- Creamy Lemon Chicken Piccata
- Garlic Herb Roast Pork Tenderloin
- Spiced Lentil Dahl
- Mediterranean Lamb Burgers
- Peanut Butter Chocolate Tart
- Updated Black Forest Cake
- Raspberry-Lemon Pavlova

Modern Meatloaf

Ingredients

- 1 lb ground beef (80/20 mix)
- 1/2 lb ground pork or turkey
- 1/2 cup breadcrumbs (panko or gluten-free)
- 1/2 cup finely chopped onions
- 2 cloves garlic, minced
- 1/4 cup grated Parmesan cheese
- 2 large eggs
- 1/4 cup unsweetened almond milk (or regular milk)
- 1/4 cup ketchup
- 1 tbsp Worcestershire sauce
- 1 tsp smoked paprika
- 1 tsp dried thyme
- 1 tsp kosher salt
- 1/2 tsp black pepper

Topping

- 1/4 cup ketchup
- 2 tbsp honey or maple syrup
- 1 tsp Dijon mustard

Instructions

1. **Preheat Oven:** Preheat your oven to 375°F (190°C). Line a baking sheet with parchment paper or use a loaf pan.
2. **Mix Ingredients:** In a large bowl, combine the ground meats, breadcrumbs, onions, garlic, Parmesan, eggs, milk, ketchup, Worcestershire sauce, smoked paprika, thyme, salt, and pepper. Mix gently until combined. Avoid overmixing to keep the loaf tender.
3. **Shape the Meatloaf:** Transfer the mixture to the prepared baking sheet and shape it into a loaf. Alternatively, press the mixture into a loaf pan.
4. **Prepare the Topping:** In a small bowl, whisk together ketchup, honey (or maple syrup), and Dijon mustard. Brush half of this mixture evenly over the meatloaf.
5. **Bake:** Place the meatloaf in the oven and bake for 40 minutes.
6. **Glaze Again:** Remove the meatloaf, brush with the remaining topping, and return to the oven. Bake for an additional 15-20 minutes, or until the internal temperature reaches 160°F (71°C).

7. **Rest and Serve:** Allow the meatloaf to rest for 10 minutes before slicing. Serve warm with your favorite sides.

Fusion Mac and Cheese

Ingredients

- 8 oz elbow macaroni
- 2 tbsp butter
- 2 tbsp all-purpose flour
- 2 cups milk
- 1 cup shredded sharp cheddar cheese
- 1/2 cup grated Parmesan cheese
- 1/4 cup crumbled feta cheese
- 1 tsp garlic powder
- 1/2 tsp smoked paprika
- 1 tbsp gochujang (Korean chili paste)
- 1/4 cup panko breadcrumbs (optional for topping)

Instructions

1. **Cook Pasta:** Boil macaroni until al dente. Drain and set aside.
2. **Make Sauce:** Melt butter in a saucepan over medium heat. Whisk in flour to create a roux. Gradually add milk, stirring constantly until thickened.
3. **Add Cheese:** Reduce heat to low. Stir in cheddar, Parmesan, feta, garlic powder, paprika, and gochujang until melted and smooth.
4. **Combine:** Toss the cooked macaroni in the sauce. Transfer to a baking dish if desired.
5. **Optional Topping:** Sprinkle with panko breadcrumbs and broil for 2-3 minutes until golden brown.

Global Chicken Pot Pie

Ingredients

- 2 cups cooked, shredded chicken
- 2 tbsp olive oil
- 1/2 cup diced onion
- 1/2 cup diced carrots
- 1/2 cup peas
- 1/2 cup diced sweet potato (optional)
- 2 tbsp all-purpose flour
- 1 cup chicken broth
- 1 cup coconut milk (or cream)
- 1 tbsp curry powder
- 1 tsp garam masala
- 1 sheet puff pastry, thawed
- 1 egg (for egg wash)

Instructions

1. **Prepare Filling:** Heat olive oil in a skillet. Sauté onions, carrots, peas, and sweet potato until softened. Add flour and stir to coat.
2. **Add Liquids and Spices:** Pour in chicken broth and coconut milk. Stir in curry powder and garam masala. Simmer until thickened. Fold in shredded chicken.
3. **Assemble Pie:** Pour the mixture into a baking dish. Lay puff pastry over the top, trimming excess. Seal edges and make small slits for ventilation. Brush with egg wash.
4. **Bake:** Preheat oven to 375°F (190°C). Bake for 25-30 minutes or until golden and puffed.

Spiced-Up Shepherd's Pie

Ingredients

- 1 lb ground lamb or beef
- 1 tbsp olive oil
- 1 cup diced onion
- 1 cup diced carrots
- 1 cup frozen peas
- 2 cloves garlic, minced
- 1 tbsp tomato paste
- 1 tsp ground cumin
- 1 tsp chili powder
- 1/2 tsp cayenne pepper (optional)
- 1 cup beef broth
- 2 lbs potatoes, peeled and boiled
- 1/4 cup butter
- 1/4 cup milk
- 1/2 cup grated cheddar cheese
- 1 tsp smoked paprika

Instructions

1. **Prepare Filling:** Heat olive oil in a skillet. Brown ground lamb or beef. Add onions, carrots, peas, and garlic. Cook until vegetables are tender. Stir in tomato paste, cumin, chili powder, and cayenne. Add beef broth and simmer until thickened.
2. **Make Mashed Potatoes:** Mash boiled potatoes with butter, milk, cheddar cheese, and paprika.
3. **Assemble Pie:** Spread the meat mixture into a baking dish. Top with mashed potatoes, spreading evenly.
4. **Bake:** Preheat oven to 375°F (190°C). Bake for 20-25 minutes or until the top is golden.

Deconstructed Lasagna

Ingredients

- 1 lb lasagna noodles, broken into large pieces
- 1 lb ground beef or sausage
- 2 cups marinara sauce
- 1 cup ricotta cheese
- 1 cup shredded mozzarella cheese
- 1/4 cup grated Parmesan
- Fresh basil, for garnish

Instructions

1. Cook the lasagna noodles until al dente.
2. Brown the ground beef in a skillet and stir in marinara sauce.
3. Layer the components on plates: noodles, meat sauce, ricotta dollops, mozzarella, and Parmesan. Garnish with fresh basil.

Reimagined Caesar Salad

Ingredients

- 1 head romaine lettuce, charred on a grill
- 1/4 cup Caesar dressing
- 1/4 cup shaved Parmesan
- 1/2 cup croutons
- 1 soft-boiled egg, halved
- Anchovy fillets (optional)

Instructions

1. Grill the romaine lettuce for a smoky flavor.
2. Arrange on a platter with dressing, Parmesan, croutons, egg, and anchovies.

Smoky Beef Stroganoff

Ingredients

- 1 lb beef sirloin, sliced thinly
- 1 tbsp smoked paprika
- 2 tbsp butter
- 1 cup sliced mushrooms
- 1/2 cup sour cream
- 1 cup beef broth
- Egg noodles, for serving

Instructions

1. Sear the beef with smoked paprika. Remove from pan.
2. Sauté mushrooms, add broth, and simmer. Stir in sour cream and beef. Serve over egg noodles.

Korean-Inspired Sloppy Joes

Ingredients

- 1 lb ground beef
- 1/4 cup gochujang
- 2 tbsp soy sauce
- 2 tbsp brown sugar
- 1 tsp sesame oil
- 4 brioche buns
- Kimchi, for topping

Instructions

1. Brown the beef and stir in gochujang, soy sauce, brown sugar, and sesame oil.
2. Serve on buns, topped with kimchi.

Vegan Bolognese

Ingredients

- 1 cup lentils, cooked
- 1/2 cup diced mushrooms
- 2 cups marinara sauce
- 1 tsp Italian seasoning
- Pasta of choice

Instructions

1. Sauté mushrooms, add marinara sauce, lentils, and seasoning.
2. Serve over cooked pasta.

Exotic Clam Chowder

Ingredients

- 1 lb clams, cleaned
- 1 cup coconut milk
- 1 cup vegetable broth
- 1 tsp curry powder
- 1/2 cup diced sweet potato
- 1/2 cup chopped onion

Instructions

1. Sauté onion and sweet potato. Add broth and curry powder.
2. Add clams and coconut milk; simmer until clams open.

Bold Beef Wellington

Ingredients

- 1 lb beef tenderloin
- 1/2 cup mushroom duxelles
- 1 sheet puff pastry
- Prosciutto slices
- Egg wash

Instructions

1. Wrap beef with duxelles and prosciutto. Enclose in puff pastry.
2. Brush with egg wash and bake at 400°F for 25 minutes.

Mediterranean Ratatouille

Ingredients

- 1 zucchini, sliced
- 1 eggplant, sliced
- 1 red bell pepper, sliced
- 1 cup marinara sauce
- 1 tbsp olive oil

Instructions

1. Layer vegetables over marinara in a dish. Drizzle with olive oil.
2. Bake at 375°F for 30 minutes.

French Onion Tartlets

Ingredients

- 1 sheet puff pastry, cut into circles
- 2 cups caramelized onions
- 1/2 cup Gruyère cheese, shredded

Instructions

1. Top pastry circles with onions and cheese.
2. Bake at 375°F for 15 minutes.

Elevated Tuna Casserole

Ingredients

- 1 lb pasta
- 1 can tuna
- 1 cup béchamel sauce
- 1/2 cup peas
- 1/4 cup breadcrumbs

Instructions

1. Mix pasta, tuna, sauce, and peas. Transfer to a dish.
2. Top with breadcrumbs and bake at 375°F for 15 minutes.

Spicy Chili con Carne

Ingredients

- 1 lb ground beef
- 1 cup kidney beans
- 1 cup diced tomatoes
- 2 tsp chili powder
- 1/2 tsp cayenne pepper

Instructions

1. Brown the beef. Add tomatoes, beans, chili powder, and cayenne.
2. Simmer for 30 minutes.

Global Pad Thai

Ingredients

- 8 oz rice noodles
- 2 tbsp vegetable oil
- 1 cup shrimp, chicken, or tofu
- 2 eggs, beaten
- 1 cup bean sprouts
- 1/4 cup crushed peanuts
- 3 tbsp tamarind paste
- 3 tbsp soy sauce
- 1 tbsp fish sauce
- 1 tbsp brown sugar
- Lime wedges and cilantro, for garnish

Instructions

1. Cook noodles according to package instructions. Drain and set aside.
2. Heat oil in a wok. Cook protein of choice, then add eggs and scramble.
3. Add noodles, tamarind paste, soy sauce, fish sauce, and sugar. Toss well.
4. Stir in bean sprouts and garnish with peanuts, lime, and cilantro.

Garlic Butter Chicken Alfredo

Ingredients

- 12 oz fettuccine pasta
- 2 tbsp butter
- 4 garlic cloves, minced
- 2 chicken breasts, sliced
- 1 cup heavy cream
- 1 cup grated Parmesan
- Fresh parsley, for garnish

Instructions

1. Cook pasta and set aside.
2. Heat butter in a skillet, sauté garlic, and cook chicken until golden.
3. Add cream and Parmesan, stirring until smooth. Combine with pasta and garnish with parsley.

Japanese Curry Shepherd's Pie

Ingredients

- 1 lb ground beef or lamb
- 1/2 cup diced onion
- 1/2 cup diced carrots
- 1/2 cup peas
- 1 cup Japanese curry sauce
- 2 lbs mashed potatoes

Instructions

1. Brown ground meat with onions, carrots, and peas. Stir in Japanese curry sauce.
2. Spread into a baking dish and top with mashed potatoes. Bake at 375°F for 20 minutes.

Creamy Mushroom Risotto

Ingredients

- 1 cup Arborio rice
- 4 cups chicken or vegetable broth
- 1/2 cup white wine
- 2 tbsp butter
- 1 cup sliced mushrooms
- 1/2 cup grated Parmesan

Instructions

1. Sauté mushrooms in butter. Set aside.
2. Toast rice in the same pan, add wine, and stir until absorbed. Gradually add broth, stirring constantly.
3. Stir in mushrooms and Parmesan.

Caribbean Jerk Roast Chicken

Ingredients

- 1 whole chicken
- 1/4 cup jerk seasoning
- 2 tbsp olive oil
- 1 lime, juiced
- 1 tbsp honey

Instructions

1. Rub chicken with seasoning, oil, lime juice, and honey.
2. Roast at 375°F for 1 hour or until cooked through.

Fresh Caprese Pizza

Ingredients

- 1 pizza dough
- 1/2 cup marinara sauce
- 1 cup fresh mozzarella slices
- 1/2 cup cherry tomatoes, halved
- Fresh basil leaves
- Drizzle of balsamic glaze

Instructions

1. Spread marinara on dough, top with mozzarella and tomatoes.
2. Bake at 425°F for 12-15 minutes. Add basil and balsamic glaze.

Gourmet Grilled Cheese

Ingredients

- 2 slices sourdough bread
- 1 tbsp butter
- 2 slices sharp cheddar
- 2 slices Gruyère
- Caramelized onions (optional)

Instructions

1. Butter bread and layer cheeses. Add onions if desired.
2. Grill in a skillet until golden and gooey.

Thai Red Curry Meatballs

Ingredients

- 1 lb ground chicken
- 1 tbsp red curry paste
- 1/4 cup breadcrumbs
- 1 can coconut milk
- 1 tbsp fish sauce
- 1 tbsp lime juice

Instructions

1. Mix chicken, curry paste, and breadcrumbs. Form into meatballs and cook in a skillet.
2. Simmer in coconut milk, fish sauce, and lime juice.

Spinach and Feta Spanakopita

Ingredients

- 1 lb spinach, wilted
- 1 cup crumbled feta
- 1 egg, beaten
- 1/2 cup chopped dill
- 1 package phyllo dough
- 1/4 cup melted butter

Instructions

1. Mix spinach, feta, egg, and dill.
2. Layer phyllo sheets with butter, adding filling between layers. Bake at 375°F for 25 minutes.

Sweet Potato Gnocchi

Ingredients

- 2 medium sweet potatoes
- 1 cup flour
- 1 egg
- 1/4 cup grated Parmesan
- Butter and sage, for sauce

Instructions

1. Roast sweet potatoes, mash, and mix with egg, flour, and Parmesan.
2. Form into gnocchi, boil until they float, and sauté in butter with sage.

Roasted Eggplant Moussaka

Ingredients

- 2 large eggplants, sliced
- 2 tbsp olive oil
- 1 lb ground beef or lamb
- 1 onion, diced
- 2 cups tomato sauce
- 1 tsp cinnamon
- 1 cup béchamel sauce
- 1/2 cup grated Parmesan

Instructions

1. Roast eggplant slices with olive oil until tender.
2. Cook ground meat with onion, tomato sauce, and cinnamon.
3. Layer eggplant and meat mixture in a baking dish, top with béchamel and Parmesan. Bake at 375°F for 25 minutes.

Tex-Mex Tacos al Pastor

Ingredients

- 1 lb pork shoulder, thinly sliced
- 2 tbsp achiote paste
- 1/4 cup orange juice
- 1/4 cup pineapple juice
- 1 tsp cumin
- Corn tortillas
- Pineapple chunks, diced onion, and cilantro for topping

Instructions

1. Marinate pork in achiote, juices, and cumin for 2 hours. Grill or sauté until cooked.
2. Serve on tortillas with pineapple, onion, and cilantro.

Peruvian-Inspired Ceviche

Ingredients

- 1 lb fresh white fish, cubed
- 1/2 cup lime juice
- 1/4 cup orange juice
- 1 red onion, thinly sliced
- 1 chili pepper, minced
- 1/4 cup cilantro, chopped
- Sweet potato slices, for serving

Instructions

1. Combine fish, juices, onion, chili, and cilantro. Let marinate in the fridge for 20 minutes.
2. Serve with sweet potato slices.

Pineapple Fried Rice

Ingredients

- 2 cups cooked rice
- 1 tbsp vegetable oil
- 1/2 cup diced pineapple
- 1/2 cup peas and carrots
- 2 eggs, scrambled
- 2 tbsp soy sauce
- 1 tsp curry powder

Instructions

1. Heat oil in a wok. Sauté pineapple and veggies.
2. Add rice, eggs, soy sauce, and curry powder. Stir-fry until combined.

Coconut Chicken Korma

Ingredients

- 1 lb chicken, cubed
- 2 tbsp vegetable oil
- 1 onion, diced
- 2 garlic cloves, minced
- 1 tbsp ginger, minced
- 1 tbsp curry powder
- 1 cup coconut milk
- 1/4 cup yogurt

Instructions

1. Sauté onion, garlic, and ginger in oil. Add chicken and curry powder, cooking until browned.
2. Stir in coconut milk and yogurt. Simmer for 15 minutes.

Lemongrass Pho

Ingredients

- 8 cups beef or chicken broth
- 2 stalks lemongrass, smashed
- 2-inch piece ginger, sliced
- 1 lb rice noodles
- 1/2 lb thinly sliced beef or chicken
- Bean sprouts, lime, basil, and chili for garnish

Instructions

1. Simmer broth with lemongrass and ginger for 20 minutes.
2. Cook noodles, add to bowls, and top with sliced protein. Pour hot broth over and garnish.

Cuban Sandwich Casserole

Ingredients

- 1 loaf Cuban bread, sliced
- 1/2 lb roasted pork, shredded
- 1/2 lb ham, sliced
- 1/2 lb Swiss cheese
- 1/4 cup pickles, sliced
- 1/4 cup mustard
- 1/4 cup butter, melted

Instructions

1. Layer bread, meats, cheese, and pickles in a baking dish.
2. Spread mustard and butter on top. Bake at 350°F for 20 minutes.

Greek-Style Stuffed Peppers

Ingredients

- 4 bell peppers, tops removed and seeds scooped
- 1 cup cooked rice
- 1/2 cup feta cheese
- 1/2 cup diced tomatoes
- 1/4 cup olives, chopped
- 1 tsp oregano

Instructions

1. Mix rice, feta, tomatoes, olives, and oregano. Stuff peppers with mixture.
2. Bake at 375°F for 30 minutes.

Sweet and Sour Pork Reimagined

Ingredients

- 1 lb pork, cubed
- 1/2 cup pineapple chunks
- 1 red bell pepper, diced
- 1/4 cup vinegar
- 1/4 cup sugar
- 1/4 cup ketchup
- 2 tbsp soy sauce

Instructions

1. Sauté pork until browned. Remove from pan.
2. Cook pineapple and bell pepper, then add vinegar, sugar, ketchup, and soy sauce. Simmer until thickened. Return pork and coat with sauce.

Butter Poached Lobster Rolls

Ingredients

- 4 lobster tails
- 1 cup unsalted butter
- 4 brioche rolls
- 1/4 cup mayonnaise
- 1 tbsp lemon juice
- Salt and pepper to taste

Instructions

1. Melt butter in a saucepan over low heat. Add lobster tails and poach until fully cooked.
2. Remove lobster, chop, and toss with mayonnaise, lemon juice, salt, and pepper.
3. Fill brioche rolls with the lobster mixture and serve.

Moroccan-Spiced Tagine

Ingredients

- 1 lb chicken thighs or chickpeas (for vegetarian)
- 1 tbsp olive oil
- 1 onion, sliced
- 2 garlic cloves, minced
- 1 cup diced tomatoes
- 1/2 cup dried apricots, chopped
- 1 tsp cinnamon
- 1 tsp cumin
- 1/2 tsp turmeric

Instructions

1. Heat oil in a tagine or pot, sauté onion and garlic. Add chicken or chickpeas, spices, tomatoes, and apricots.
2. Simmer covered for 30 minutes, stirring occasionally. Serve with couscous.

Middle Eastern Shakshuka

Ingredients

- 1 tbsp olive oil
- 1 onion, diced
- 1 bell pepper, diced
- 2 cups tomato sauce
- 1 tsp paprika
- 1/2 tsp cumin
- 4-6 eggs
- Parsley for garnish

Instructions

1. Sauté onion and bell pepper in oil until soft. Add tomato sauce and spices, simmer for 10 minutes.
2. Make small wells in the sauce, crack eggs into them, and cover. Cook until eggs are set. Garnish with parsley.

Pesto Zucchini Noodles

Ingredients

- 4 zucchinis, spiralized
- 1/2 cup basil pesto
- 1/4 cup grated Parmesan
- 1 tbsp olive oil

Instructions

1. Sauté zucchini noodles in olive oil for 2-3 minutes. Toss with pesto and Parmesan. Serve warm.

Tangy BBQ Pulled Jackfruit

Ingredients

- 1 can young jackfruit, drained
- 1/2 cup BBQ sauce
- 1 tbsp apple cider vinegar
- 1/2 tsp smoked paprika
- Burger buns for serving

Instructions

1. Shred jackfruit and sauté in a pan with vinegar and smoked paprika. Add BBQ sauce and simmer for 10 minutes.
2. Serve on buns as pulled jackfruit sandwiches.

French-Inspired Quiche Lorraine

Ingredients

- 1 pie crust
- 6 slices bacon, cooked and crumbled
- 1 cup shredded Gruyère cheese
- 3 eggs
- 1 cup heavy cream
- Salt and pepper to taste

Instructions

1. Preheat oven to 375°F. Line a pie dish with crust.
2. Whisk eggs, cream, salt, and pepper. Layer bacon and cheese in the crust, pour egg mixture over.
3. Bake for 35-40 minutes until set.

Chorizo and Black Bean Stew

Ingredients

- 1 lb chorizo, sliced
- 1 can black beans, drained
- 1 onion, diced
- 1 cup diced tomatoes
- 1 tsp smoked paprika
- 1/2 tsp cumin

Instructions

1. Sauté chorizo and onion until browned. Add beans, tomatoes, and spices.
2. Simmer for 15 minutes, stirring occasionally.

Sweet Potato Shepherd's Pie

Ingredients

- 1 lb ground beef or lentils
- 1 onion, diced
- 2 cups mixed vegetables (carrots, peas, etc.)
- 2 cups mashed sweet potatoes
- 1/2 cup beef or vegetable broth
- 1 tbsp tomato paste

Instructions

1. Cook ground beef or lentils with onion. Add vegetables, broth, and tomato paste. Simmer for 10 minutes.
2. Spread mixture in a baking dish, top with mashed sweet potatoes. Bake at 375°F for 20 minutes.

Chili Lime Shrimp Tacos

Ingredients

- 1 lb shrimp, peeled and deveined
- 2 tbsp lime juice
- 1 tsp chili powder
- Corn tortillas
- Toppings: shredded cabbage, avocado, cilantro

Instructions

1. Marinate shrimp in lime juice and chili powder for 15 minutes. Sauté or grill until cooked.
2. Serve on tortillas with desired toppings.

Creamy Lemon Chicken Piccata

Ingredients

- 4 chicken breasts, pounded thin
- 1/2 cup all-purpose flour
- 3 tbsp olive oil
- 1 cup chicken broth
- 1/2 cup heavy cream
- 1/4 cup lemon juice
- 2 tbsp capers
- Parsley for garnish

Instructions

1. Dredge chicken in flour and sear in olive oil until golden, then set aside.
2. Deglaze the pan with chicken broth, stir in cream, lemon juice, and capers. Simmer for 5 minutes.
3. Return chicken to the pan and cook until done. Garnish with parsley.

Garlic Herb Roast Pork Tenderloin

Ingredients

- 1 pork tenderloin (about 1.5 lbs)
- 3 garlic cloves, minced
- 2 tbsp olive oil
- 1 tsp dried rosemary
- 1 tsp dried thyme
- Salt and pepper to taste

Instructions

1. Preheat oven to 400°F. Rub tenderloin with garlic, herbs, olive oil, salt, and pepper.
2. Roast for 20-25 minutes until the internal temperature reaches 145°F. Rest for 5 minutes before slicing.

Spiced Lentil Dahl

Ingredients

- 1 cup red lentils
- 1 onion, diced
- 2 garlic cloves, minced
- 1 tsp turmeric
- 1 tsp cumin
- 1 tsp curry powder
- 2 cups vegetable broth

Instructions

1. Sauté onion and garlic in oil until fragrant. Add spices and toast briefly.
2. Stir in lentils and broth. Simmer for 20 minutes, stirring occasionally, until lentils are soft.

Mediterranean Lamb Burgers

Ingredients

- 1 lb ground lamb
- 1/4 cup breadcrumbs
- 2 garlic cloves, minced
- 1 tsp oregano
- Salt and pepper to taste
- Toppings: tzatziki, tomato slices, arugula
- Burger buns

Instructions

1. Mix lamb, breadcrumbs, garlic, oregano, salt, and pepper. Form into patties.
2. Grill or pan-sear until cooked to desired doneness. Serve on buns with toppings.

Peanut Butter Chocolate Tart

Ingredients

- 1 pre-made tart crust
- 1 cup creamy peanut butter
- 1/2 cup powdered sugar
- 1 cup heavy cream
- 8 oz dark chocolate, chopped

Instructions

1. Mix peanut butter and powdered sugar until smooth. Spread into the tart crust.
2. Heat cream until hot, pour over chocolate, and whisk until smooth. Pour over peanut butter layer. Chill until set.

Updated Black Forest Cake

Ingredients

- 1 chocolate sponge cake
- 2 cups whipped cream
- 1 cup cherry pie filling
- Dark chocolate shavings for garnish

Instructions

1. Layer chocolate cake with whipped cream and cherry filling.
2. Frost with whipped cream and garnish with chocolate shavings.

Raspberry-Lemon Pavlova

Ingredients

- 4 egg whites
- 1 cup sugar
- 1 tsp cornstarch
- 1 tsp lemon juice
- 1 cup whipped cream
- 1 cup fresh raspberries
- Zest of 1 lemon

Instructions

1. Preheat oven to 250°F. Whisk egg whites until stiff peaks form, gradually add sugar, cornstarch, and lemon juice.
2. Spread into a circle on parchment paper and bake for 1 hour. Cool completely.
3. Top with whipped cream, raspberries, and lemon zest.

www.ingramcontent.com/pod-product-compliance
Lightning Source LLC
LaVergne TN
LVHW081324060526
838201LV00055B/2444